CZECHOSLOVAK TEXTILES

The object of this series is to present a Survey of World Textiles, each volume dealing with a separate country. The undermentioned are either published or in course of preparation.

Other volumes are to follow and will be announced from time to time.

CZECHOSLOVAK TEXTILES

by

FRANK LEWIS

F. LEWIS, PUBLISHERS, LIMITED

LEIGH-ON-SEA

PRINTED AND MADE IN ENGLAND

©
Copyright by
F. LEWIS, PUBLISHERS, LIMITED
Leigh-on Sea, England

First published 1962

Printed at The Dolphin Press, Brighton

Introduction

THE MANUFACTURE of Textiles in Czechoslovakia is as old as the history of the country. Its tradition resembles a magic ball, the thread of which takes us back to the ancient times of a thousand years ago. In the Book of Kingdoms and Travel compiled by Al Bekri in the 12th century we can find an account by an Arab merchant, Ibrahim ibn Yakoub, dated about 950 A.D., running somewhat as follows:—

> 'In the country called Buyama (Bohemia) they make light-weight scarves of very fine material. Their price is 10 scarves for one kin-shar (denarius). Any goods may be bought for these scarves and they serve to express the value of all things. They can be exchanged for wheat, flour, horses, gold, silver, and all else'.

This news may be more than a thousand years old, but textiles have remained an outstanding product of Czechoslovak industry to this day.

Of course, it is no longer only light-weight scarves and fine linen that are made here. To the old-established linen-making industry there was added, in the 15th century, a lively wool cloth production and later also hat-making. Shortly after the first cotton was brought to Europe a number of cotton mills and cotton printing plants arose on the territory of present-day Czechoslovakia. Their products soon found their way to many countries of Europe and overseas.

The present-day picture of the Czechoslovak textile industry is as full of interest as a glance into its past. Apart from the traditional manufacture of woollen and worsted fabrics, of cotton goods, and of hats, there is a rich selection of silk and rayon fabrics, textile prints, furnishing fabrics and carpets, lace, hosiery goods, underwear, and ready-made clothes. Numerous well-equipped plants grouped in larger units of national corporations remain true to old-established traditions binding present-day workers to continue the good work of their predecessors. They make use, however, of all facilities provided by up-to-date technique to improve continually the process of manufacture so as to keep abreast of the latest developments in the world.

The great care paid by the socialist industries to the education of young textile workers and to their technical training, pleasant and healthy working conditions in the works, and continuous improvement of production methods all tend to make the high standard of Czechoslovak textiles even higher.

Their numerous lines, as for example Czechoslovak poplins, fancy-woven handkerchiefs, linen damasks, furnishing gobelins, guipure lace, and many others have become just another word for high-quality goods.

Special attention is paid to designing in which prominent artists take an active part. The manufacturing concerns co-operate closely with the Institute of Interior and Fashion Design (UBOK) and with the Arts and Crafts School in Prague. The latter supplies industry with designers who are well prepared for creative work in the textile branch.

The results of this co-operation can be seen in all textile ranges, which are outstanding not only for the richness of their designs and high fashion qualities, but also for their characteristic artistic styling.

When speaking about Czechoslovak textiles, it is not sufficient to mention only their production. The story of their export is no less fascinating.

As early as 1428 mention was made of the first sale of Czech cloth to the Linz market. In the 16th century Czech linen and wool cloth were exported regularly to foreign countries in horse-drawn wagons.

With its large-scale mechanization of textile production the 19th century brought about a remarkable growth of exports. Textile mills built on the territory of present-day Czechoslovakia supplied their products not only to the whole of the Austro-Hungarian Monarchy, but also to many other European countries, and they found their way even to other continents.

At present, all imports and exports of textiles are in the hands of a single concern, the foreign trade corporation of *Centrotex* in Prague, which maintains business contacts with all countries of the world and organizes displays of Czechoslovak textiles at all important international fairs.

The range of textiles made in Czechoslovakia is extremely rich and the following pages can give only a general idea.

COTTON FABRICS

These hold first place among Czechoslovak textiles both as to their wide production range and their fame. High-quality raw material, especially Egyptian cotton, is made into well-known poplins for shirts, dresses and pyjamas, sports shirtings, dress materials, raincoat materials, fine handkerchiefs, terry towelling, sheetings, mattress tickings, corduroys, and many other lines of high-quality goods.

THE MANUFACTURE OF LINEN GOODS

This oldest branch of the Czechoslovak textile industry, has centuries-old experience which manifests itself in the fineness and hard-wearing qualities of all its products. On one hand, the modern industry puts on the market its traditional goods—table cloths and table sets, damasks, napkins, towels, and bed linen, while on the other hand, it pays attention to new lines, such as sunshade and deckchair cloths, dress materials, tailors' cloths, printed furnishing fabrics, etc.

WORSTED AND WOOLLEN GOODS

Those made in Czechoslovakia belong to a category of textiles that have won world-wide fame for their standard quality. The good work of weavers and designers has left its mark both on fine worsted fabrics made with the application of complex weaving techniques and on fashionable woollen materials. An important branch of the wool industry is the production of plushes and astrakhans, which introduces every season many tasteful novelties.

FURNISHING FABRICS

Czechoslovakia has an advanced production of carpets and furnishing fabrics. Carpets are made in a rich assortment of woollen, pile and jute types. The range of furnishing fabrics is also very rich, including both classical gobelins and modern materials from wool, cotton, and man-made fibres.

TEXTILE PRINTS

These are made in Czechoslovakia by all printing methods. Printed textiles include faultlessly made machine prints on cotton and spun rayon, screen prints on cotton, silk, rayon and silon, and block prints on wool known as hand-printed cashmeres.

The long years of export experience of the printing mills has resulted in a wealth of designs that can meet the requirements and tastes of all world markets.

LACE, TULLE AND CURTAINS

These dainty textiles supply proof of the high level of technical skill of the Czechoslovak textile industry. Fineness, neatness of design and good quality of the material—these are the main features of all kinds of Czechoslovak lace products, whether it be guipure narrow and all-over lace, lace made on Leaver's machines, valenciennes, bone lace, embroidered cambric, or other kinds of curtain materials.

RIBBONS, TRIMMINGS, THREADS AND YARNS

These minor but very important goods are made in highly specialized works with an old tradition in manufacture and export. Their products include dress, lingerie and hat ribbons, elastic ribbons, braids of every description, tinsel ware, threads and imitation silk threads for industry and the home, and, finally, embroidery and knitting yarns of well-known brands.

HATS, FEZCAPS AND BERETS

It is more than 160 years ago that the first hat factory was established in Czechoslovakia. Since then a big industry has developed which turns out high quality hats and semi-finished hatters' products. The production of fezcaps and berets has also a long tradition and supplies of these go to many foreign markets.

READY-MADE CLOTHES AND UNDERWEAR

These have a long tradition which has grown from good tailoring shops and old-established textile mills. The common features of all these products are accurate and neat craftsmanship and high quality of the fabrics used.

Up-to-date clothing factories make suits and dresses, raincoats, weather-resisting jackets, corduroy clothes, men's shirts, pyjamas, and every kind of underwear and lingerie.

KNITWEAR AND HOSIERY

The Czechoslovak production of knitwear has registered a remarkable growth in the course of recent years. Up-to-date knitting mills closely follow world fashion and constantly enlarge the range of their products. They make all kinds of outer and underwear from wool, cotton, rayon and man-made fibres. Excellent results have been achieved in the production of nylon stockings and socks featuring good hard-wearing qualities. Let us also mention gloves, the range of which includes many types of both textile and leather lines.

FELTS AND TECHNICAL TEXTILES

In Czechoslovakia these goods are afforded ever greater attention as they find ready use in many industries both at home and abroad. Special types of felts are made for paper mills, for the engineering, leather goods, textile, chemical and foodstuffs industries, for making musical instruments, and for clothing factories. Czechoslovakia also possesses an outstanding production of industrial cloths, tarpaulins, artificial leather, glass yarns, glass-fibre textiles, and many other technical textiles used in various industries and in the building trade.

Descriptive Notes
on the Illustrations

Figures 1 and 2 (*Left*) Surface detail of a bouclé structural carpet. (*Right*) Surface detail of a bouclé carpet with cut pile. From MORAVAN n.p.[1], Brno.

Figures 3 and 4 (*Left*) A woollen double-plush carpet made of worsted yarns with an oriental design. (*Right*) A double-plush carpet made of carded yarns with oriental design. From TOKO n.p., Vratislavice.

Figure 5 A bouclé carpet. From MORAVAN n.p., Brno.

Figure 6 A hand-knotted carpet. From ÚBOK[2], Praha.

Figure 7 Design for machine woven pile carpet. From TOKO n.p., Vratislavice.

Figure 8 Design for machine woven carpet. From TOKO n.p., Vratislavice.

Figure 9 A machine woven pile carpet with a Persian design. From TOKO n.p., Vratislavice.

Figures 10 and 11 (*Top*) A hand-knotted rug. From ÚBOK, Praha. (*Bottom*) Czechoslovak carpets exhibited from Centrotex at the 1960 exhibition in Moscow.

1. See notes p. 20
2. See notes p. 20

Figures 12 and 13   (*Left*) Gobelin Tapestry '*Queen of Hearts*' by Antonin Kybal which was awarded the GRAND PRIX at the Brussels World Fair of 1958. (*Right*) Gobelin Tapestry '*Twilight in a painter's studio*', by Antonin Kybal, 1956.

Figures 14 and 15   (*Top*) The weaving of the Gobelin tapestry '*Czech Hunting Game*' designed by Jiří Fusek. Awarded the GRAND PRIX at the Brussels Exposition 1958. Woven at the VŠUP, Praha. (*Bottom*) A Gobelin tapestry '*PRAHA—the Mother of Cities*' designed by Jos. Müller. Size: 3 by 4 metres. Woven at the VŠUP, Praha.

Figure 16   Curtain material, screen printed in one colour. From ÚBOK, Praha.

Figure 17   A two colour screen printed cotton curtaining. From ÚBOK, Praha

Figures 18 and 19   (*Left*) Curtaining material, screen printed in two colours on cotton. From ÚBOK, Praha. (*Right*) This decorative fabric is a four colour screen print on cotton. From DÍLO, Praha.

Figures 20 and 21   (*Left*) A curtaining fabric, screen printed in three colours on artificial silk. (*Right*) This decorative fabric is also a three colour screen print, but on cotton. Both from ÚBOK, Praha.

Figures 22 and 23   (*Top*) Three colour screen printed curtaining material on artificial silk. (*Bottom*) Screen printed cotton in three colours. Both from ÚBOK, Praha.

Figures 24 and 25   (*Top*) A curtaining fabric, a one colour screen print. From DÍLO, Praha. (*Bottom*) Two and three colour screen printed cotton curtaining materials. From ART HANDICRAFT, Praha (Umělecka řemesla).

Figures 26 A decorative two colour screen printed cotton from DÍLO, Praha.

Figures 27 and 28 (*Top*) A Jacquard pure silk taffeta dress fabric for ladies evening wear. From HEDVA n.p., Mor. Třebová. (*Bottom*) This is a ladies dress material, screen printed in three colours on nylon and comes from ÚBOK, Praha.

Figures 29 and 30 (*Top*) A pure silk taffeta dress material, made for fine evening wear— Jacquard woven. From HEDVA n.p., Mor. Třebová. (*Bottom*) A ladies dress material, screen printed in one colour on silk—the illustration showing two patterns in the same design, one lighter and the other in a darker shade. From TIBA, n.p., Dvůr Králové n./L.

Figures 31 and 32 (*Top*) A one colour machine printed cotton dress fabric. From Tiba n.p., Dvůr Králové n./L. (*Bottom*) Ladies dress fabric, screen printed in three colours on silon. From ÚBOK, Praha.

Figures 33 and 34 (*Top*) This dress fabric is a multi-coloured print on cotton featuring a floral motive. From TIBA, n.p., Dvür Králové n./L.

Figures 35 and 36 (*Top*) This ladies dress fabric, a three colour printed cotton in a design with a strawberry motive. From TIBA n.p., Dvůr Králové n./L. (*Bottom*) This is a three colour printed cotton dress fabric with a rose motive and also comes from TIBA n.p.

Figures 37 and 38 (*Left*) A multi-coloured hand-blocked cashmere scarf. From TEX-TILANA n.p., Liberec. (*Right*) A silk scarf in a gaily coloured print from TIBA n.p., Dvůr Králové n./L.

Figure 39 Detail of a fine cashmere scarf, hand-blocked and multi-coloured. From TEXTILANA, n.p., Liberec.

Figures 40 to 43 (*Top Left and Right*) Two three colour screen printed cashmere scarves. These were exhibited at the Brussels International Exhibition 1958 and were awarded a GRAND PRIX. From TEXTILANA, n.p., Liberec. (*Bottom Left*) a silk scarf, screen printed in four colours. From TIBA n.p. (*Bottom Right*) A decorative silk scarf, a four colour print with a spring motif. This particular scarf was also awarded a GRAND PRIX at the Brussels Internation Exhibition of 1958. From TIBA n.p., Dvůr Králové n/L.

Figures 44 and 45 (*Left*) A decorative linen fabric, double-faced, in a multi-coloured jacquard design. (*Right*) Decorative fabric with a linen warp and weft of artificial silk, in a jacquard design. Both are from TEXLEN n.p., Trutnov.

Figures 46 and 47 (*Left*) A decorative one colour screen printed fabric on linen. From TEXLEN, n.p., Trutnov. (*Right*) This is a decorative, one colour screen printed linen fabric. From ÚBOK, Praha. (Institute of Interior and Fashion Design).

Figures 48 to 51 (*Top Left*) A decorative two colour screen print on linen. From TEXLEN, n.p., Trutnov. (*Top Right and bottom Left*) Two decorative screen printed linen fabrics in one colour. From ÚBOK, Praha. (*Bottom Right*) A three coloured screen printed curtain fabric. From ÚBOK, Praha.

Figures 52 and 53 (*Left*) Ladies dress fabric, a multi-coloured print on cotton. From TIBA n.p., Dvůr Králové n./L. (*Right*) Decorative curtain fabric with a jacquard woven design. From PLYŠAN n.p., Hlinsko.

Figures 54 and 55 (*Top*) Gent's worsted suitings. (*Bottom*) Samples of ladies dress materials made of carded yarns. Both from VHJ[3] Vlna, Brno.

---

3. See notes p. 20

Figures 56 and 57   Furnishing fabrics with small jacquard designs. Spun rayon or cotton warp with woollen or blended weft. From TOKO, n.p., Vratislavice.

Figures 58 and 59   A further selection of furnishing materials in small jacquard designs. Spun rayon or cotton warp with woollen or blended weft. From TOKO, n.p., Vratislavice.

Figures 60 and 61   Two-faced woollen furnishing fabrics with jacquard designs. Produced at VŠUP, Praha. (College of Applied Art).

Figure 62   A cotton jacquard furnishing fabric with a plant design. From ÚBOK, Praha

Figures 63 and 64   (*Top*) Printed woollen plushes—'a fur fantasy'. From VELVETA, n.p., Varnsdorf. (*Bottom*) Two-face woollen furnishing fabrics with jacquard designs. Produced at VŠUP, Praha. (College of Applied Art).

Figure 65   Samples of ladies and gent's woollen coatings, made of carded yarn. From VHJ Vlna, Brno.

Figures 66 and 67   (*Top*) Samples of ladies and gent's suit and costume fabrics of combed and carded yarn. From VHJ Vlna, Brno. (*Bottom*) Cotton blankets of the APIS brand. From VHJ Bytový textil, Vratislavice.

Figures 68 and 69   (*Top*) Samples of gent's suitings made of both carded and combed yarns. (*Bottom*) Samples of ladies' costume and coat fabrics made of combed yarn. Both from VHJ Vlna, Brno.

Figures 70 and 71 (*Top*) Fancy woven cotton shirtings with sateen stripes and cross weaves. (*Bottom*) A further selection of fancy woven cotton fabrics for gent's sports shirts and ladies' blouses. Both from VHJ Bavlna, Hradec Králové.

Figure 72 Cotton sports shirtings with fancy woven designs. From VHJ Bavlna, Hradec Králové.

Figures 73 and 74 (*Top*) Ladies' dress material made of cotton, fancy woven in a crease resistant finish. (*Below*) Gent's shirtings made of fine cotton. Fancy woven designs with many woven-in effects. Shrink and crease resistant finish. Both from VHJ Bavlna, Hradec Králové.

Figures 75 and 76 (*Left*) Dress and pyjama poplins with fancy woven designs on light and medium dark grounds. (*Right*) Dress and pyjama cotton fabrics. Fancy woven designs executed in various interesting weaving techniques. Both from VHJ Bavlna, Hradec Králové.

Figures 77 and 78 (*Left*) A ladies' cotton dress material, fancy woven, with contrasting sateen stripes. (*Right*) Also a cotton dress material with a fancy woven design on a white ground. Both from VHJ Bavlna, Hradec Králové.

Figures 79 and 80 Cotton Terry fabrics, piece woven and printed in four colours. From VEBA n.p., Police n/Metují and TIBA n.p., Dvůr Králové.

Figures 81 and 82. (*Top*) Cotton Terry bath-towels with fancy woven plastic designs. From VEBA n.p., Police n/Metují. (*Bottom*) A piece woven cotton terry fabric, printed in four colours. From VEBA n.p., Police n/Metují and TIBA n.p., Dvůr Králové.

Figures 83 and 84   (*Top*) A fancy woven linen table cloth from TEXLEN, n.p., Trutnov. (*Bottom*) This fancy woven linen table-cloth comes from MORAVOLEN, n.p., Šumperk.

Figures 85 and 86   (*Top*) A linen table-cloth with a printed floral motif. (*Bottom*) A detail of a multi-coloured printed table-cloth designed by K. Svolinský. Both from TIBA, n.p., Dvůr Králové n/Labem.

Figures 87 and 88   (*Top*) Gent's cotton handkerchiefs, fancy woven in subtle colours. (*Bottom*) A cotton handkerchief with an original design on a dark ground. From MILETA n.p., Hořice v Podkrkonoší.

Figures 89 and 90   (*Top*) Cotton ladies' handkerchiefs with non-symmetrical fancy woven designs. (*Bottom*) These too, are fancy woven and in fine pastel shades. All from MILETA n.p., Hořice v Podkrkonoší.

Figures 91 to 94   Mattress tickings with a cotton warp and linen weft. From TEXLEN n.p., Trutnov.

Figures 95 and 96   (*Top*) A handkerchief trimmed with lace. (*Bottom*) Examples of decorative galloons. Both from KRAJKA n.p., Kraslice.

Figures 97 and 98   (*Top*) Several examples of embroidered cambrics manufactured in various shades. (*Bottom*) Samples of airy guipure allover lace dress materials. All from KRAJKA n.p., Kraslice.

Figures 99 to 101   (*Top*) Embroidered monofile from KRAJKA n.p., Kraslice. (*Centre*) Hand made bone lace: '*A folklore procession*' made according to a drawing. Awarded a Gold Medal at the Brussels International Exhibition of 1958. Produced by the VAMBERECKA KRAJKA CO-OPERATIVE. (*Bottom*) Embroidered cambric from KRAJKA n.p., Kraslice.

Figure 102   Samples of embroidered monofile, From KRAJKA n.p., Kraslice.

Figure 103   Bone and Valenciennes laces. From TYLEX n.p., Letovice.

Figures 104 to 108   Samples of cotton curtaining. All from TYLEX n.p., Letovice.

Figures 109 and 110   (*Top*) Taffeta ribbons with check designs. (*Bottom*) Jacquard ribbons for National costumes, with multi-coloured folklore designs. All from STUHY a PRÝMKY, n.p. Vilemov.

NOTES

1. N.P. or n.p.   Abbreviation for Národní Podnik or national enterprise.

2. UBOK   Institute of Interior and Fashion Design. The abbreviated letters stand for the Czech style and name.

3. VHJ   Abbreviation for Production, Centre which include a number of mills of the same type of production, i.e. woollen and woollen products, cotton and cotton products, etc.

ILLUSTRATIONS

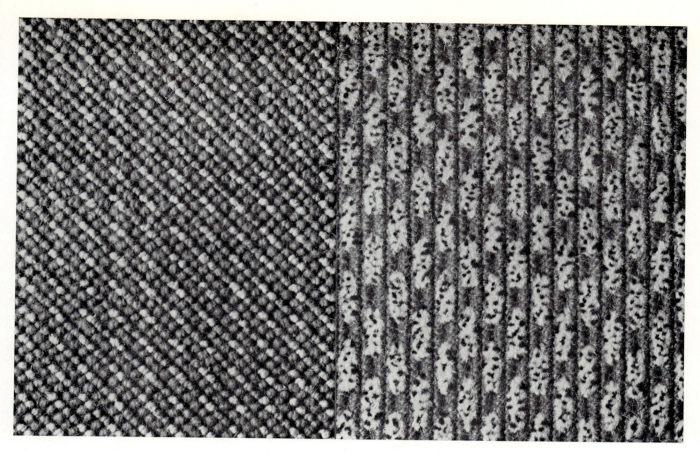

FIG. 1/2. FROM MORAVAN N.P., BRNO

FIG. 3/4. FROM TOKO N.P., VRATISLAVICE

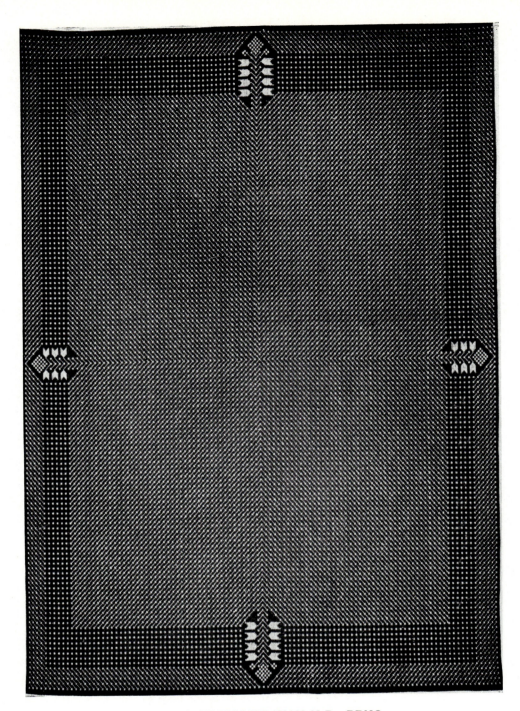

FIG. 5. FROM MORAVAN N.P., BRNO

FIG. 6. FROM ÚBOK, PRAHA

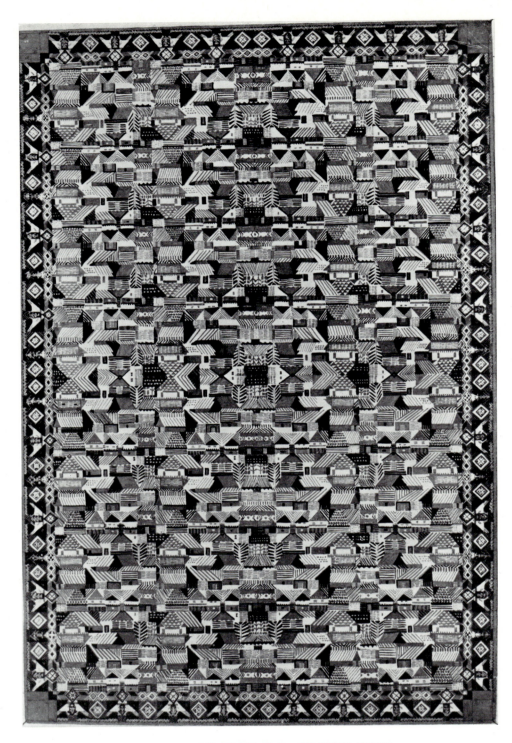

FIG. 7. FROM TOKO N.P., VRATISLAVICE

FIG. 8. FROM TOKO N.P., VRATISLAVICE

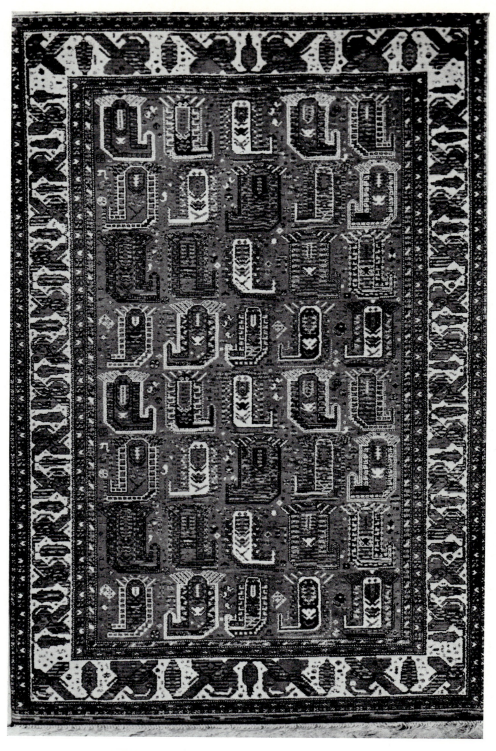

FIG. 9. FROM TOKO N.P., VRATISLAVICE

FIG. 10/11. *(top)* FROM ÚBOK, PRAHA *(bottom)* FROM CENTROTEX, PRAHA

FIG. 12/13. BY ANTONIN KYBAL

FIG. 14/15. FROM VŠUP, PRAHA

FIG. 16. FROM ÚBOK, PRAHA

FIG. 17. FROM ÚBOK, PRAHA

FIG. 18/19. *(left)* FROM ÚBOK, PRAHA *(right)* FROM DÍLO, PRAHA

FIG. 20/21. FROM ÚBOK, PRAHA

FIG. 22/23. FROM ÚBOK, PRAHA

FIG. 24/25. *(top)* FROM DÍLO, PRAHA *(bottom)* FROM ART HANDICRAFT, PRAHA

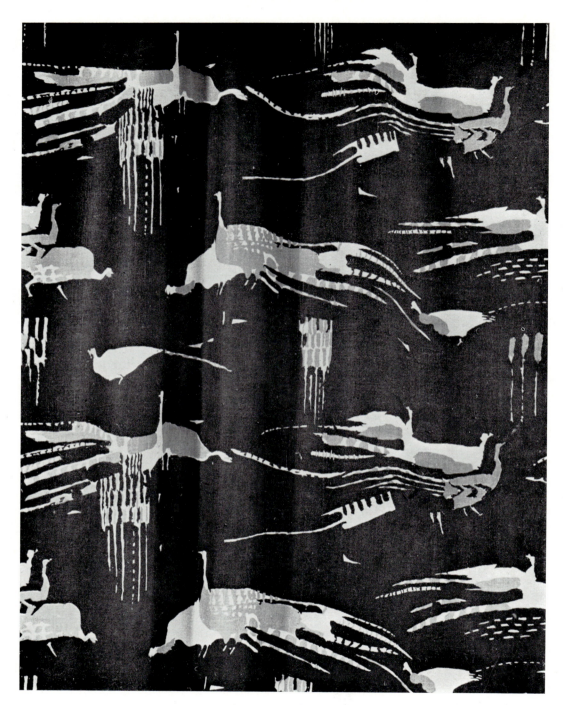

FIG. 26. FROM DÍLO, PRAHA

FIG. 27/28. *(top)* FROM HEDVA N.P., MOR. TŘEBOVÁ *(bottom)* FROM ÚBOK, PRAHA

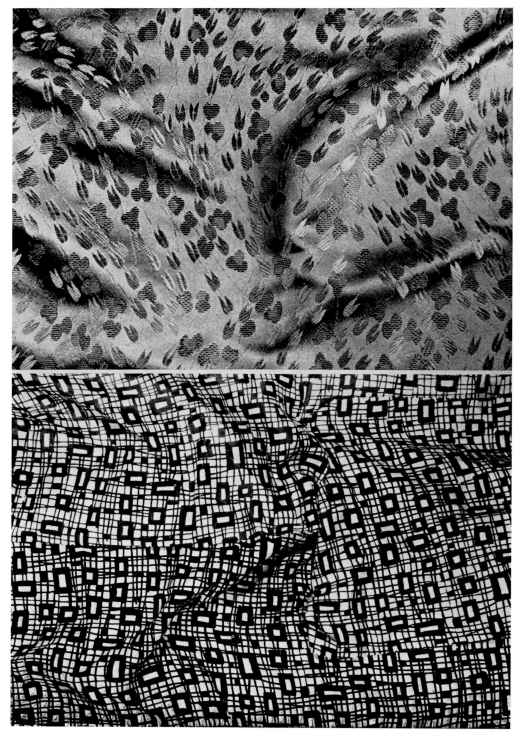

FIG. 29/30. *(top)* FROM HEDVA N.P., MOR. TŘEBOVÁ *(bottom)* FROM TIBA N.P.,
DVŮR KRALOVÉ N/L

FIG. 31/32. *(top)* FROM TIBA N.P., DVŮR KRÁLOVÉ N/L *(bottom)* FROM ÚBOK, PRAHA

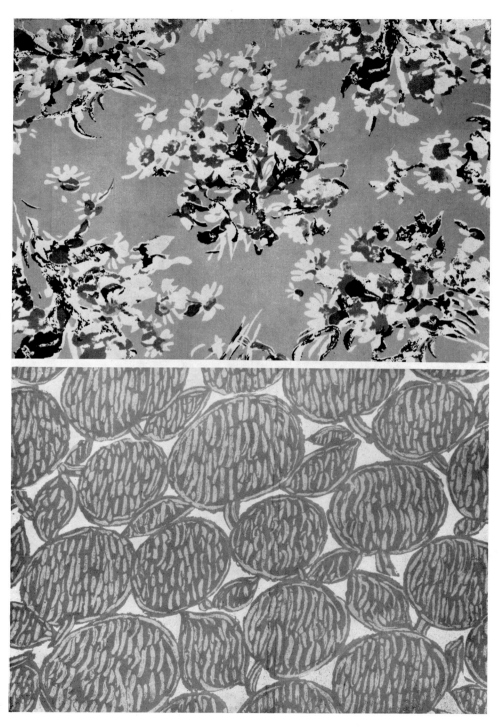

FIG. 33/34. FROM TIBA N.P., DVŮR KRÁLOVÉ N/L

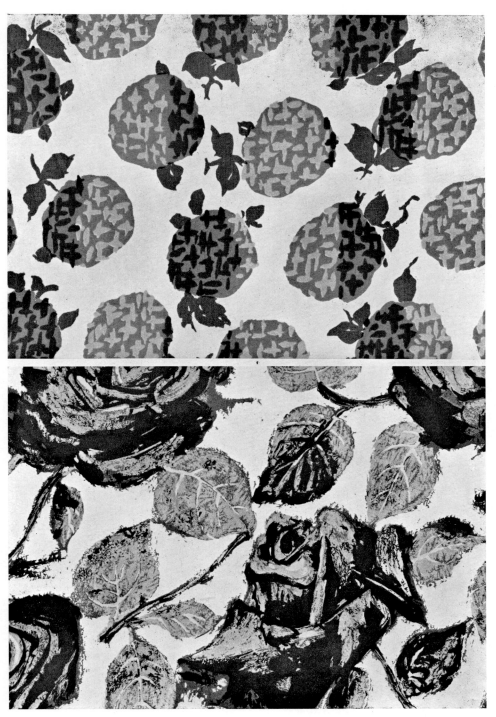

FIG. 35/36. FROM TIBA N.P., DVŮR KRÁLOVÉ N/L

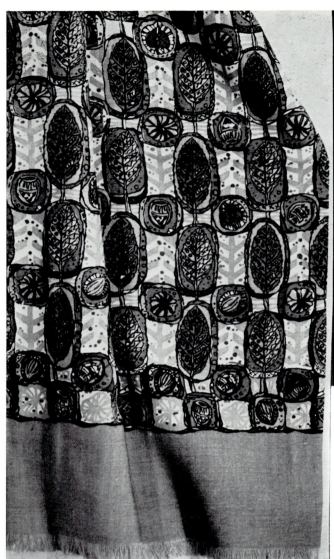

FIG. 37/38. *(left)* FROM TEXTILANA N.P., LIBEREC *(right)* FROM TIBA N.P., DVŮR KRÁLOVÉ N/L

FIG. 39. FROM TEXTILANA N.P., LIBEREC

FIG. 40/43. *(top left and right)* FROM TEXTILANA N.P., LIBEREC *(bottom left and right)* FROM TIBA N.P., DVŮR KRÁLOVÉ N/L

FIG. 44/45. FROM TEXLEN N.P., TRUTNOV

FIG. 46/47. *(left)* FROM TEXLEN N.P., TRUTNOV *(right)* FROM ÚBOK, PRAHA

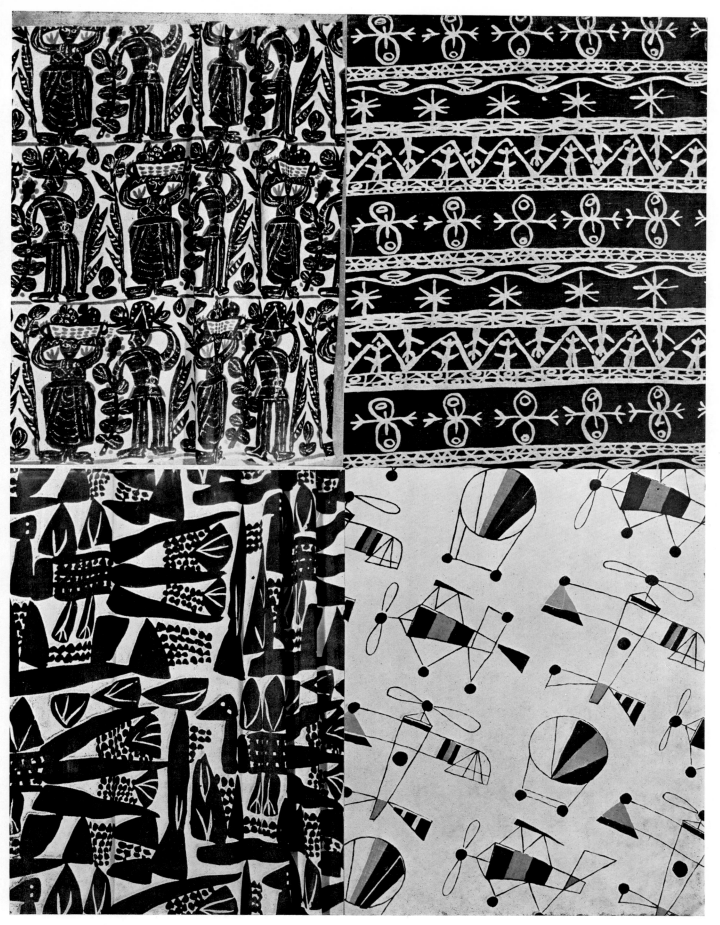

FIG. 48/51. *(top left)* FROM TEXLEN N.P., TRUTNOV. *(top right and bottom left and right)* FROM ÚBOK, PRAHA

FIG. 52/53. *(left)* FROM TIBA N.P., DVŮR KRÁLOVÉ N/L *(right)* FROM PLYŠAN N.P., HLINSKO

FIG. 54/55. FROM VHJ VLNA, BRNO

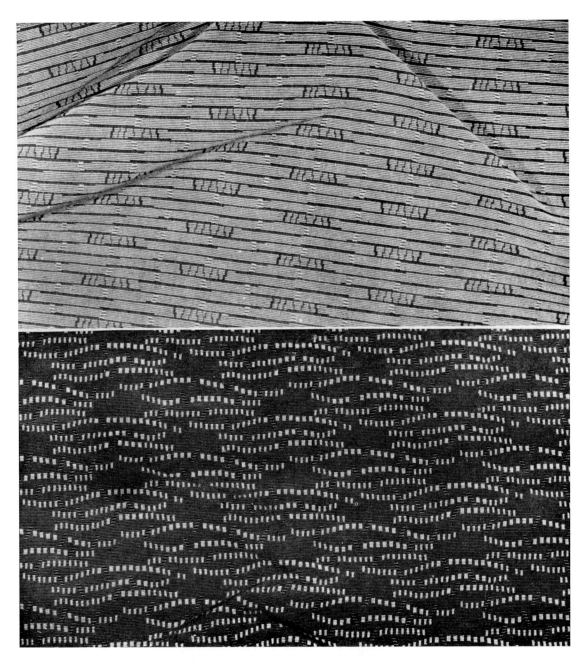

FIG. 56/57. FROM TOKO N.P., VRATISLAVICE

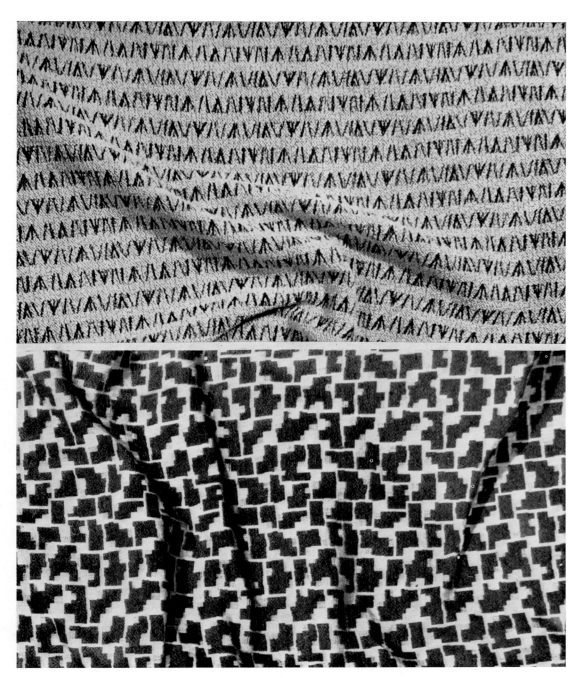

FIG. 58/59. FROM TOKO N.P., VRATISLAVICE

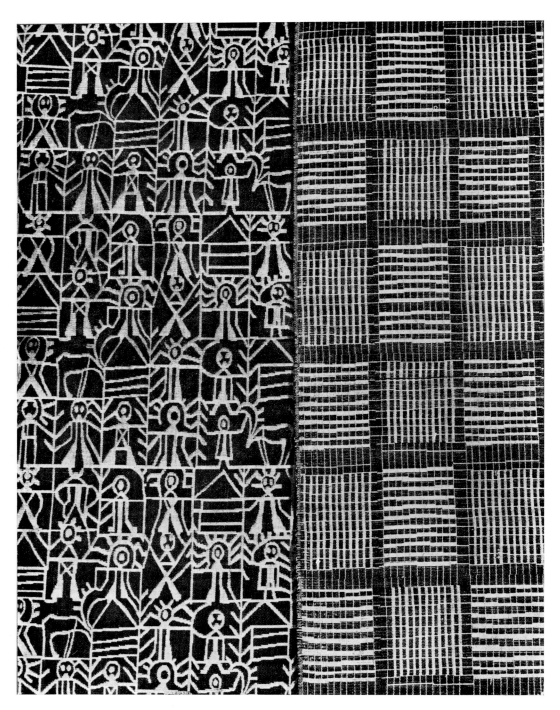

FIG. 60/61. FROM VŠUP, PRAHA

FIG. 62. FROM ÚBOK, PRAHA

FIG. 63/64. *(top)* FROM VELVETA N.P., VARNSDORF *(bottom)* FROM VŠUP,

PRAHA

FIG. 65. FROM VHJ VLNA, BRNO

FIG. 66/67. *(top)* FROM VHJ VLNA, BRNO *(bottom)* FROM VHJ BYTOVÝ

TEXTIL, VRATISLAVICE

FIG. 68/69. FROM VHJ VLNA, BRNO

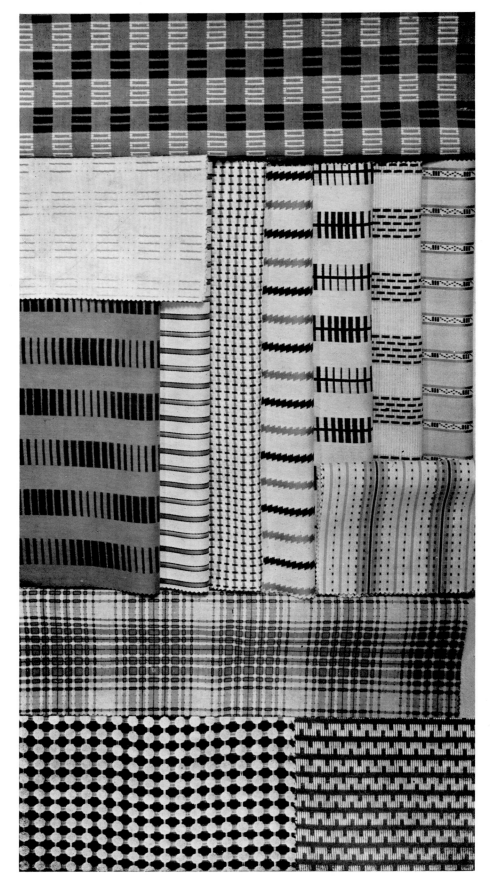

FIG. 70/71. FROM VHJ BAVLNA, HRADEC KRÁLOVÉ

FIG. 72. FROM VHJ BAVLNA, HRADEC KRÁLOVÉ

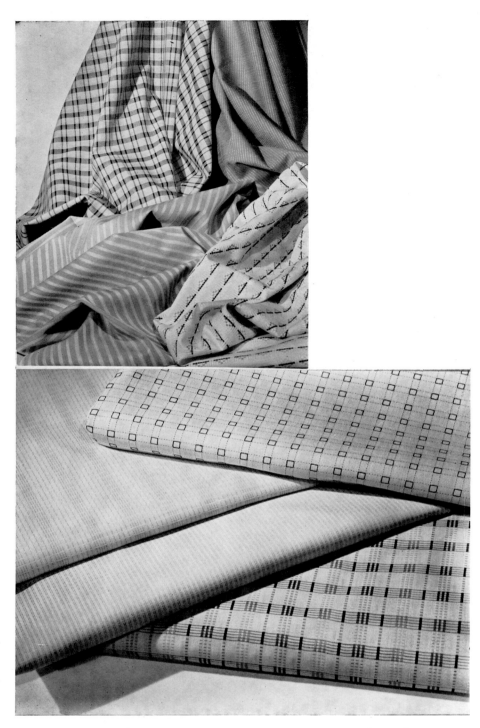

FIG. 73/74. FROM VHJ BAVLNA, HRADEC KRÁLOVÉ

FIG. 75/76. FROM VHJ BAVLNA, HRADEC KRÁLOVÉ

FIG. 77/78. FROM VHJ BAVLNA, HRADEC KRÁLOVÉ

FIG. 79/80. FROM VEBA N.P., POLICE N/METUJÍ AND TIBA N.P., DVŮR
KRÁLOVÉ

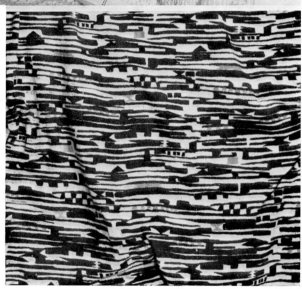

FIG. 81/82. FROM VEBA N.P., POLICE N/METUJÍ

FIG. 83/84. *(top)* FROM TEXLEN N.P., TRUTNOV *(bottom)* FROM
MORAVOLEN, N.P., ŠUMPERK

FIG. 85/86. FROM TIBA N.P., DVŮR KRÁLOVÉ

FIG. 87/88. FROM MILETA N.P., HOŘICE V PODKRKONOŠÍ

FIG. 89/90. FROM MILETA N.P., HOŘICE V PODKRKONOŠÍ

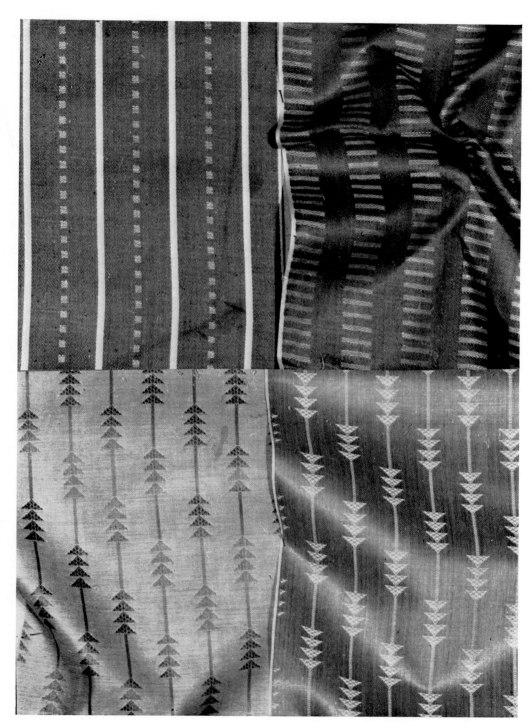

FIG. 91/94. FROM TEXLEN N.P., TRUTNOV

FIG. 95/96. FROM KRAJKA N.P., KRASLICE

FIG. 97/98. FROM KRAJKA N.P., KRASLICE

FIG. 99/101. *(top and bottom)* FROM KRAJKA N.P., KRASLICE *(centre)* FROM THE
VAMBERECKA KRAJKA CO-OPERATIVE

FIG. 102. FROM KRAJKA N.P., KRASLICE

FIG. 103. FROM TYLEX N.P., LETOVICE

FIG. 104/108. FROM TYLEX N.P., LETOVICE

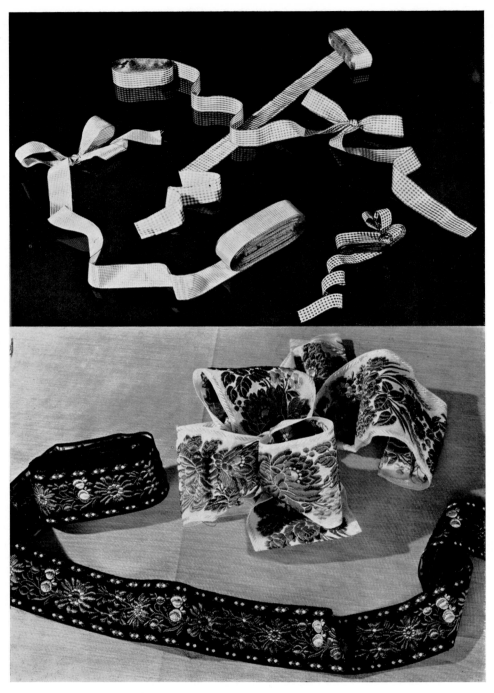

FIG. 109/110. FROM STUHY A PRÝMKY N.P., VILÉMOV

BELGIAN TEXTILES

The object of this series is to present a Survey of World Textiles, each volume dealing with a separate country.

Other volumes are to follow and will be announced from time to time

BELGIAN
TEXTILES

by

FRANK LEWIS

F. LEWIS, PUBLISHERS LIMITED

LEIGH-ON-SEA, ENGLAND

PRINTED AND MADE IN ENGLAND

©
Copyright by
F. LEWIS (PUBLISHERS) LIMITED
Leigh-on-Sea, England
SBN 85317 028 2

First published 1975

Printed at Dædalus Press, Stoke Ferry, Norfolk

Introduction

THE PRESENT VOLUME is not in any way intended to be the last word, but its objective is to obtain and present to the reader a representative collection of post-war Belgian textiles, the 22nd volume in this series, each dealing with a separate country, which give a fair *Survey of World Textiles Today*.

The attainment of this objective presented difficulties and the results are subject to limitations and qualifications – simple striped and plain fabrics have for the most part been omitted, with the emphasis throughout being on *Design*.

Thus, in introducing BELGIAN TEXTILES, it is as well to bear in mind its compact size, a population of less than ten million people, settled in an area one-quarter the size of New York State, but being blessed with some natural resources, and what is rather important, a hard-working people.

Its history is wrapped in that of the Low Countries of which it formed part for a very long period in time, in fact Belgium as such, starts from 1830, when the southern part of the Low Countries separated from the North, and two Kingdoms, Belgium and the Netherlands came into being.

Belgium has always been renowned for its linen industry, it was in the year 782 that Charlemagne (742-814) decreed that this ancient craft be revived by growing flax, spinning and weaving linen. The River Lys which flows through Courtrai, was found to contain a natural chemical vital to the separation of the flax fibre from the stalks. The cloudy, rainy weather of the district also proving ideal for the raising of fine tall plants. Today this medieval City, in the Flemish part of Belgium, is the centre of the flax and linen industry, producing linen draperies, sheer casements, wall coverings, slip-covers, upholstery and kindred furnishing fabrics, table linen, kitchen towels in a variety of weaves and weights.

The Belgian textile industry exports almost the whole of her production to markets scattered throughout the world, her home market being comparatively small. It is interesting to note here that Belgian productions cannot be said to have a National character, but only what is 'Made in Belgium' – the designs primarily for the export markets – her carpets for instance are mainly oriental in concept, not mere reproductions of originals, but more an interpretation. Many types do not even have an 'international character', but only character of the market for which they are almost exclusively meant, for instance prayer rugs or mats produced for the near and middle East in cheap qualities. Some modern designs are however produced.

Like the Netherlands, Belgium had to build up and develop an entirely independent industry – former Belgian Colonies having been lost to the wave of independence sweeping the world presenting great problems at the time, but these have been overcome.

Fashion textiles, in both natural and man-made fibres, constitute today a very considerable portion of the industry, as do the wool fabrics, which include suitings for men's wear.

So today, Belgian textiles, the product of science and the creative spirit of her designers and weavers, have taken their proper place in this modern world of highly competitive markets.

Descriptive Notes
on the Illustrations

Figure 1   ELEPHANTS. Curtain fabric on a satin ground. The design being obtained with a Rayon Broche or needlework effect. Inspired from an embroidered hanging of the early 17th century. (Edmond Meert S.A., St. Nicolas-Waas).

Figure 2   TRUNKS. Damask (Damasse) ground with crackled effect, ornamented with panel representing a rustic winter scene, and developed by the intermixing of more weave effects so as to obtain the photo-like appearance it has. (Edmond Meert S.A., St. Nicolas-Waas).

Figure 3   SEVRES PORCELAIN. Curtaining fabric, very particular and original in its conception and technique; it was carefully studied to obtain a precise picture of the design suggesting figurines in Porcelain of Sevres. (Edmond Meert S.A., St. Nicolas-Waas).

Figure 4   ORCHARD.   This very decorative fabric, that may answer for quite a number of purposes, is enlightened in colours illuminating the whole. The design suggesting all the charm of an orchard in blossom. (Edmond Meert S.A., St. Nicolas-Waas).

Figure 5   FLOWER DAMASK. A curtaining fabric. Damask with multi-coloured nosegays of flowers, the colours enhancing the whole. (Edmond Meert S.A., St. Nicolas-Waas).

Figure 6   A silk fabric with the ground in a linen weave effect, with the design being formed with broche effect. The texture, design and colours producing all the charm of the past, of which it recalls the beloved flower-basket so artistically developed in the silk fabrics of the 18th century. (Edmond Meert S.A., St. Nicolas-Waas).

Figure 7   An adaptation of the well known stripe patterns of the 18th century. This is a curtaining or an upholstery fabric. Between straight stripes in satin weave effect in self colour ribbons are baskets of flowers and the famous true lover's knot. (Edmond Meert S.A., St. Nicolas-Waas).

Figure 8   ACROPOLE. A curtain damask. The design inspired by Grecian columns, running down between self colour satin stripes. (Edmond Meert S.A., St. Nicolas-Waas).

Figure 9   BRANCHES & FLOWERS. A curtaining fabric. Wavy satin ground which is typical of this textile, the design being formed with set off effect in both old and glittering gold. (Edmond Meert S.A., St. Nicolas-Waas).

Figure 10   BROCADE. An upholstery fabric. A period design on a ground glittering through the interlace of different wefts. (Edmond Meert S.A., St. Nicolas-Waas).

Figure 11   BROCATELLE. Curtain and upholstery fabric. A deep ground with a set off satin counterground, ornamented with multi-coloured sprays of flowers and leaves obtained in broche weave. (Edmond Meert S.A., St. Nicolas-Waas).

Figure 12   SPRAY OF FLOWERS. An upholstery fabric. The whole surface is cut by stems in a multitude of small ogival compartments each with a tapestry woven spray in the centre on a twill woven ground, the stems enframing and enhancing rep ground. (Edmond Meert S.A., St. Nicolas-Waas).

Figure 13   VERDURE. A beautiful and luxurious tapestry, the very clever colour arrangements highlighting the whole. (Edmond Meert S.A., St. Nicolas-Waas).

Figure 14   SWEET PEAS. Multi-coloured nosegays of Sweet Peas on a satin ground comprise this curtain material. (Edmond Meert S.A., St. Nicolas-Waas).

Figure 15   REVONTULI. This furnishing fabric was designed by Marjatta Metsovaara. (S.A. Albert Van Havere, St. Niklaas).

Figure 16   Inspired from an Empire period silk fabric. (Soc. Anon. des Ern. De Witte-Visage, Marcke-lez-Courtrai).

Figures 17 *and* 18   Two woven furnishing fabrics relying entirely on their textured effects. They both achieve a fine decorative effect. (Etabs. Marchant & Stichelmans S.A. Termonde).

Figure 19   This sumptuous silk Damask inspired from an early 18th century example and typical of the elegance of the period —the Golden Age as far as design was concerned. (Soc. Anon. des Etab. Ern De Witte-Visage., Marcke-lez-Courtrai).

Figure 20   Linen curtaining No. 9934. Designed by J. Coppens. (Tissage De Gryse-Facon, Ronse).

Figure 21   Linen curtaining No. 632. Designed by J. Coppens and made by Tissage De Gryse-Facon, Ronse.

Figure 22   Belgian linen drapery fabric in which the black and white nubbly thread creates a wonderful effect. (Vve L. Tant, Roulers).

Figure 23   This decorative 100% linen fabric comes from Vve L. Tant of Roulers.

Figure 24   GROS FILS. This 100% Belgian linen decorative fabric has a wave of white and ecru threads making it a very effective design. Can be used for light draperies. (Rene Van Doorne & Cie, Eeklo).

Figure 25   Jacquard woven table carpet. (Tissage et Teinturerie Sagaert Freres, Zandberg, Harelbeke).

Figure 26   MUSIC. A jacquard woven material. (Tissage et Teinturerie Sagaert Freres, Zandberg, Harelbeke).

Figure 27   Ornamental silk screen (Batik method used). (Made and designed by Jacqueline Schepens, Brussels 5).

Figure 28   Another Batik-printed ornamental silk screen. (Made and designed by Jacqueline Schepens, Brussels 5).

Figure 29   This tapestry is a reproduction, mechanically woven, after the unrivalled set of 12 Flander Tapestries of the 16th century, representing the Maximillian Hunting scenes. Each bear the Zodiac signs, corresponding to the twelve months of the year and represent the great coursings in the Brussels country and the Woods of Soignies. The Dukes of Brabant had their hunting Lodge there, and at the fringe of the Wood the Ter-Vuerin Castle, their summer residence. The models for this set of tapestries are ascribed to Bernard Van Orley (Brussels *c.* 1487-1541). In the Musée du Louvre since the 17th Century. The reproduction here is the Falconry (start) under the sign of the Ram. The scenery shows the Castle of the town of Brussels; to left the towers of Saint-Jacques and the Hotel de Ville and the Saint-Nicolas tower (which collapsed in 1714); to extreme left the Cathedral of St. Michel. (Kunstweverij Ter Waes, St. Nicolas-Waas).

Figure 30   FALCONRY. This wall panel was taken from a tapestry representing the Maximillian Hunting scenes (see fig. 29) created in the Brussels factories in the 16th century. (Kunstweverij Ter Waes, St. Nicolas-Waas).

Figure 31   FLORE. Goddess of Flowers and Gardens receiving the fruits of the Earth. After a painting by Jan Breughel and Henry Van Balen. (Kunstweverij Ter Waes, St. Nicolas-Waas).

Figure 32   VERDURE TAPESTRY. A picturesque landscape scene in wooded country. (Edmond Meert S.A., St. Nicolas-Waas).

Figure 33   Entitled THE RIDE, this mechanically woven tapestry is an excellent rendering in the modern manner of an historical scene. (Edmond Meert S.A., St. Nicolas-Waas).

Figure 34   VERDURE & HERONS. This has been taken from a wall panel that was, according to all probability, manufactured in the factories of either Audenaerde or Tourna at the end of the 15th or early 16th century. (Edmond Meert S.A., St. Nicolas-Waas).

Figures 35, 36, 37, 38   Four modern wall panels entitled SUSSEX FARM 1443/1; COUNTRY INN 1444 L/1; and a pair of pastoral scenes numbers 596/8. (Photos courtesy of 'Febeltex', the Federation De L'Industrie Textile Belge, Brussels).

Figure 39   PALMETTE FOLIAGE CARPET. Inpsired by a Persian carpet of the 17th century. A conspicuous feature is the large and gracefully curving lanceolate leaf, where it is further distinguished by the fluidity and perfect naturalism of the drawing. (Edmond Meert S.A., St. Nicolas-Waas).

Figure 40   VASE CARPET. This carpet was inspired from a 17th century Persian (Ispahan) carpet. The field is cut by one set of stems into distinct ogival compartments in different colours and with a major palmette in the centre. In this carpet the stem is employed to define a marquetry of polychrome cartouches of exceptional beauty. (Edmond Meert S.A., St. Nicolas-Waas).

Figure 41   Wool reproduction rug, inspired by the Arab rugs from Firdaus in Persia and the surrounding area. (Algemene Fluweelweverij N.V., Courtrai).

Figure 42   SILVEX No. 5084. One of the many oriental reproductions from this firm. (Manufacture Franco Belge de Tapis S.A., Wevelgem).

Figure 43   SAROUK 9011. This is a very interesting carpet, all the borders being filled with animals and horsemen. (Manufacture Franco Belge de Tapis S.A., Wevelgem).

Figure 44   Reminiscent of the lovely Persian Garden carpets, from which this reproduction wool carpet is obviously inspired. (Algemene Fluweelweverij N.V., Courtrai).

Figures 45, 46, 47, 48   Cotton rugs for the bedroom and bathroom. (Edmond Meert S.A., St. Nicolas-Waas).

Figure 49   BIRD. Designed by Zuster Jacqueline and made by J. Van Vaerenbergh, (Kantschool Zusters Ursulinen, St. Truiden).

Figure 50   BIRD. Lace designed by L. Velter and made by J. Van Vaerenbergh, (Kantschool Zusters Ursulinen, St. Truiden).

Figure 51   CHILD. Designed by Zuster Scholastica and made by L. Lambrechts (Kantschool Zusters Ursulinen, St. Truiden).

Figures 52, 53, 54   Three pictures of lacework made and designed by Jan Deckx of Brussels.

Figure 55   QUEBEC. A table cloth of linen and cotton. (Etabs. Textiles Gerard Waelkens of Pittem).

Figure 56   LINZ. A linen and cotton mixture fabric for table cloths. This example is in soft pastel colours. (Etabs. Textiles Gerard Waelkens, Pittem).

Figure 57   100% Belgian linen tablecloth with an outstanding design of sunflowers. (Vve L. Tant of Roulers).

Figure 58   This double damask table cloth comes with a very elegant scroll border and centre piece. (Etabs. Abbeloos & Fils de Ghent).

Figure 59   Belgian linen table cloth in light woven checks in varying colours. (Solintext of Courtrai).

Figure 60   This Belgian linen table cloth has a jacquard woven floral decoration of cotton – the result is very pleasing. (Tissage La Flandre).

Figure 61   MADEIRE. Designed and made in the manufacturers' own studio and factory. (Textiles De Witte-Lietaer, Lauwe-bij-Kortrijk).

Figure 62   CALVI is the name given to this table cloth, again made and designed in the makers' factory. (Textiles De Witte- Lietaer, Lauwe-bij-Kortrijk).

Figure 63   Hand-woven woollen bedspread. Designed and made by S. Docquier of Brussels.

Figure 64   MANTACRIL in Tivoli pattern. A blanket designed by Monique Dupuis. Acribel, a new material for blankets, is warm, lightweight, mothproof, washes in cold water, quick drying, does not shrink or become matted. (Manta S.A., Waasmunster).

Figure 65   RHOVYL. A very warm satin-bound blanket. (Manta S.A., Waasmunster).

Figure 66   A selection of printed and embroidered sheets. All designed by Chloe de Bruneton. (S.A. de Waerschoot, Waerschoot).

Figure 67   MARGUERITE. Sheets designed and made by U.C.O., Ledeberg (Ghent).

Figures 68, 69, 70   Three children's Cot Blankets from a range produced by S.A. Manta, Waasmunster.

Figure 71   From the range of Etabs A. Van Damme S.A., of Eeklo, come these wool and worsted piece goods for men's suitings. These are in pure wool and wool mixed with man-made fibres.

Figure 72   Woollens designed for sports jackets and winter coatings. (Etabs. A. Van Damme, of Eeklo).

Figure 73   Cosmetic purses, toilet bags and beach bags designed and made by Combeli, Brussels.

Figure 74   Three handkerchiefs from the range of Tissages Holvoet-Van Outryve et Lagae & Fils.

Figure 75   Belgian linen kitchen towels. Produced from designs by Vera of New York. 100% Belgian linen. (Texis, Brussels).

Figure 76   DRAKKAR. This printed cotton, available in various colours, comes from Etabs. Attout-Soenens of Brussels.

Figure 77   POPULAGES. A printed cotton fabric in various colourings. (Etabs. Attout-Soenens, of Brussels).

Figure 78　A delightfully fresh and Spring-like print of scattered bouquets of flowers on a white ground. (Indienneries Belges S.A. of Ghent).

Figure 79　A simple all-over flower print (Indienneries Belges S.A. of Ghent).

Figure 80　Cotton fabrics from the firm of S.A. Louters of Ghent whose Mills were established as far back as 1790. This range is known under the trade name of 'Coriandre'.

Figure 81　A modern contemporary-designed cotton print addressed mainly to the Eastern and African markets. (Indienneries Belges S.A. of Ghent).

Figure 82　Vari-coloured printed dress fabrics. (Indienneries Belges S.A. of Ghent).

FIGURE 1. EDMOND MEERT S.A., ST. NICOLAS-WAAS

FIGURE 2. EDMOND MEERT S.A., ST. NICOLAS-WAAS

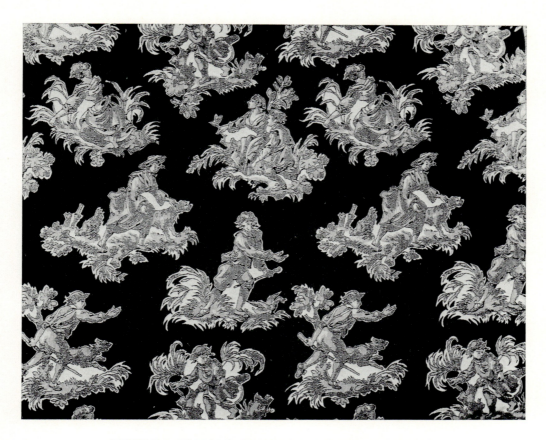

FIGURE 3. EDMOND MEERT S.A., ST. NICOLAS-WAAS

FIGURE 4. EDMOND MEERT S.A., ST. NICOLAS-WAAS

FIGURE 5. EDMONT MEERT S.A., ST. NICOLAS-WAAS

FIGURE 6. EDMOND MEERT S.A., ST. NICOLAS-WAAS

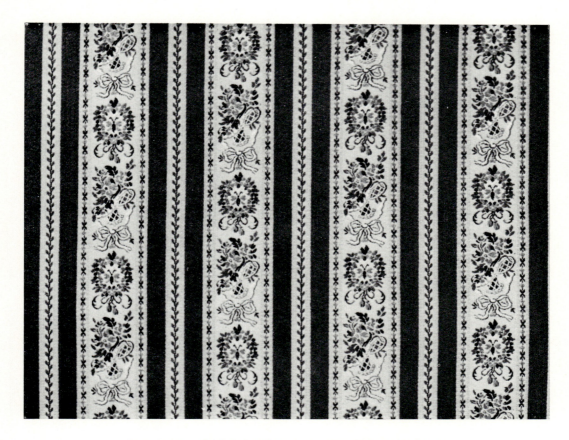

FIGURE 7. EDMOND MEERT S.A., ST. NICOLAS-WAAS

FIGURE 8. EDMOND MEERT S.A., ST. NICOLAS-WAAS

FIGURE 9. EDMOND MEERT S.A., ST. NICOLAS-WAAS

FIGURE 10. EDMOND MEERT S.A., ST. NICOLAS-WAAS

FIGURE 11. EDMOND MEERT S.A., ST. NICOLAS-WAAS

FIGURE 12. EDMOND MEERT S.A., ST. NICOLAS-WAAS

FIGURE 13. EDMOND MEERT S.A., ST. NICOLAS-WAAS

FIGURE 14. EDMOND MEERT S.A., ST. NICOLAS-WAAS

FIGURE 15. S.A. ALBERT VAN HAVERE, ST. NIKLAAS

FIGURE 16. S.A. ETABS. ERN. DE WITTE-VISAGE, MARCKE-LEZ-COURTRAI

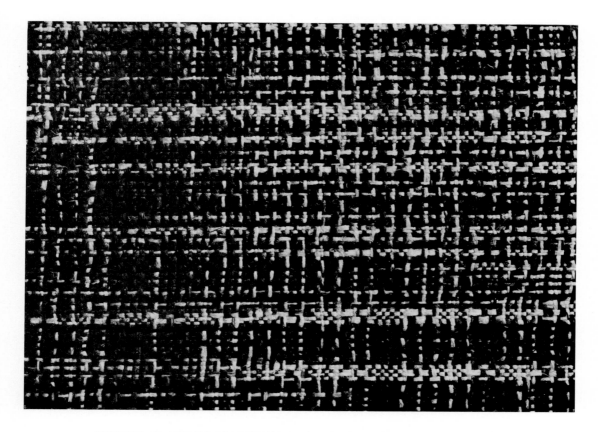

FIGURE 17. ETABS. MARCHANT & STICHELMANS S.A., TERMONDE

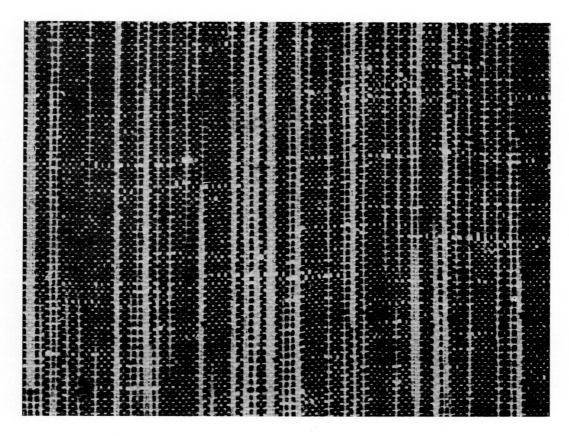

FIGURE 18. ETABS. MARCHANT & STICHELMANS S.A., TERMONDE

FIGURE 19. S.A. ETABS. ERNE DE WITTE-VISAGE, MARCKE-LEZ-COURTRAI

FIGURE 20. TISSAGE DE GRYSE-FACON, RONSE

FIGURE 21. TISSAGE DE GRYSE-FACON, RONSE

FIGURE 22. VVE L. TANT, ROULERS

FIGURE 23. VVE L. TANT, ROULERS

FIGURE 24. RENE VAN DOORNE & CIE, EEKLO

FIGURE 25. TISSAGE ET TEINTURERIE SAGAERT FRERES, ZANDBERG, HARELBEKE

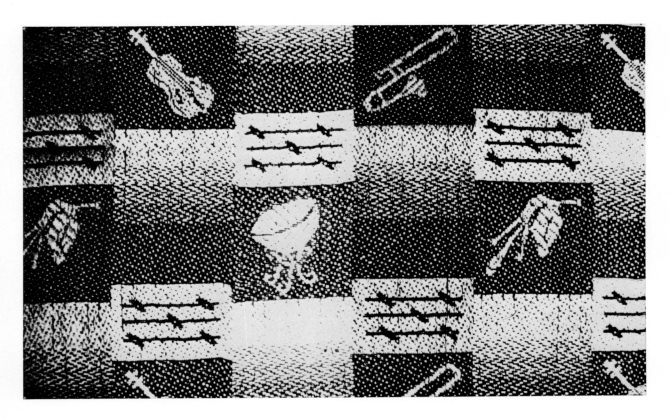

FIGURE 26. TISSAGE ET TEINTURERIE SAGAERT FRERES, ZANDBERG, HARELBEKE

FIGURE 27. JACQUELINE SCHEPENS, BRUSSELS

FIGURE 28. JACQUELINE SCHEPENS, BRUSSELS

FIGURE 29. KUNSTWEVERIJ TER WAES, ST. NICOLAS-WAAS

FIGURE 30. KUNSTWEVERIJ TER WAES, ST. NICOLAS-WAAS

FIGURE 31. KUNSTWEVERIJ TER WAES, ST. NICOLAS-WAAS

FIGURE 32. EDMOND MEERT S.A., ST. NICOLAS-WAAS

FIGURE 33. EDMOND MEERT S.A., ST. NICOLAS-WAAS

FIGURE 34. EDMOND MEERT S.A., ST. NICOLAS-WAAS

FIGURE 35. PHOTOGRAPH COURTESY OF FEBELTEX, BRUSSELS

FIGURE 36. PHOTOGRAPH COURTESY OF FEBELTEX, BRUSSELS

FIGURE 37. PHOTOGRAPH COURTESY OF FEBELTEX, BRUSSELS

FIGURE 38. PHOTOGRAPH COURTESY OF FEBELTEX, BRUSSELS

FIGURE 39. EDMOND MEERT S.A., ST. NICOLAS-WAAS

FIGURE 40. EDMOND MEERT S.A., ST. NICOLAS-WAAS

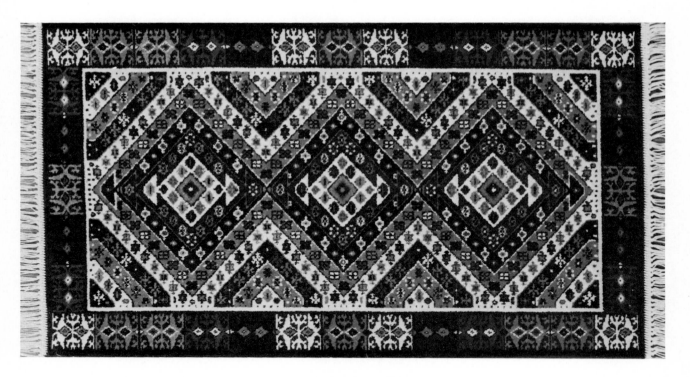

FIGURE 41. ALGEMENE FLUWEELWEVERIJ N.V., COURTRAI

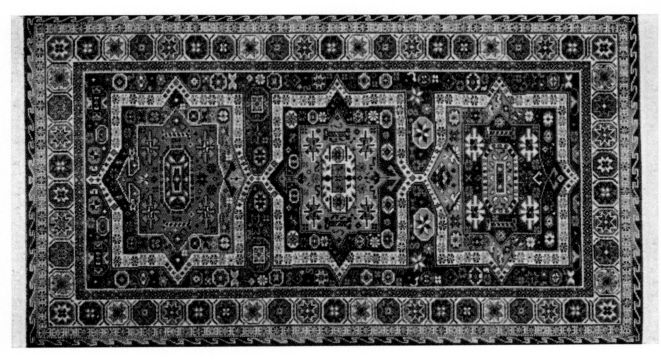

FIGURE 42. MANUFACTURE FRANCO BELGE DE TAPIS S.A., WEVELGEM

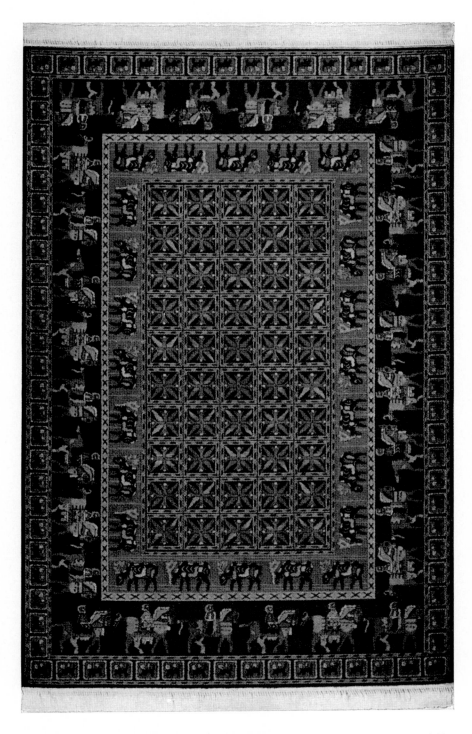

FIGURE 43. MANUFACTURE FRANCO BELGE DE TAPIS S.A., WEVELGEM

FIGURE 44. ALGEMENE FLUWEELWEVERIJ N.V., COURTRAI

FIGURE 45. EDMOND MEERT S.A., ST. NICOLAS-WAAS

FIGURE 46. EDMOND MEERT S.A., ST. NICOLAS-WAAS

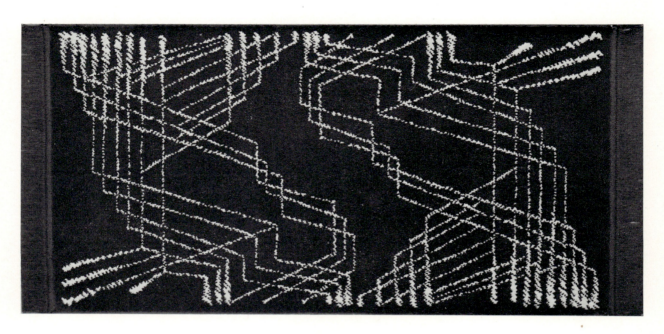

FIGURE 47. EDMOND MEERT S.A., ST. NICOLAS-WAAS

FIGURE 48. EDMOND MEERT S.A., ST. NICOLAS-WAAS

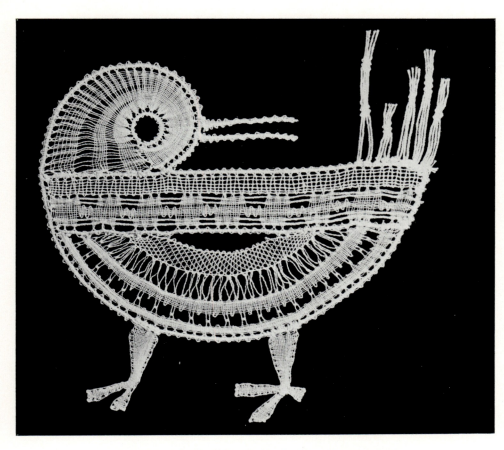

FIGURE 49. J. VAN VAERENBERGH, ST. TRUIDEN

FIGURE 50. J. VAN VAERENBERGH, ST. TRUIDEN

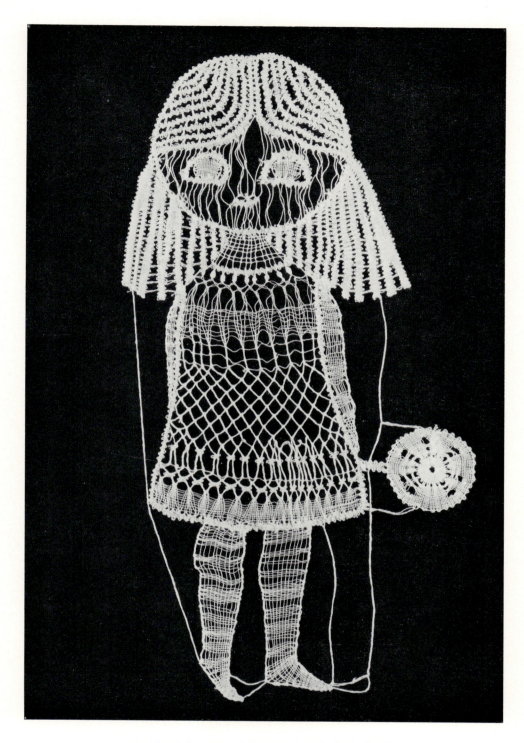

FIGURE 51. L. LAMBRECHTS, ST. TRUIDEN

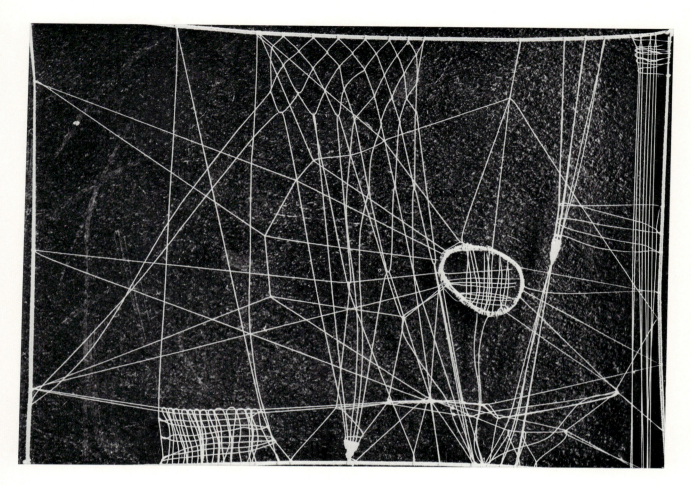

FIGURE 52. JAN DECKX, BRUSSELS

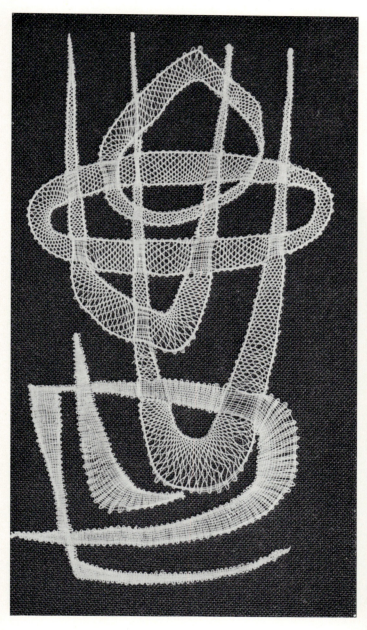

FIGURE 53. JAN DECKX, BRUSSELS

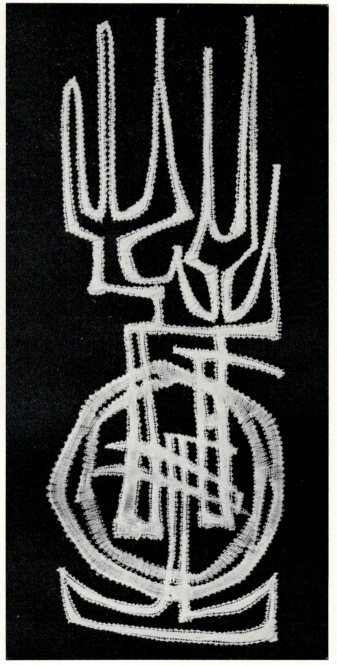

FIGURE 54. JAN DECKX, BRUSSELS

FIGURE 55. ETABS. TEXTILES GERARD WAELKENS, PITTEM

FIGURE 56. ETABS. TEXTILES GERARD WAELKENS, PITTEM

FIGURE 57. VVE L. TANT, ROULERS

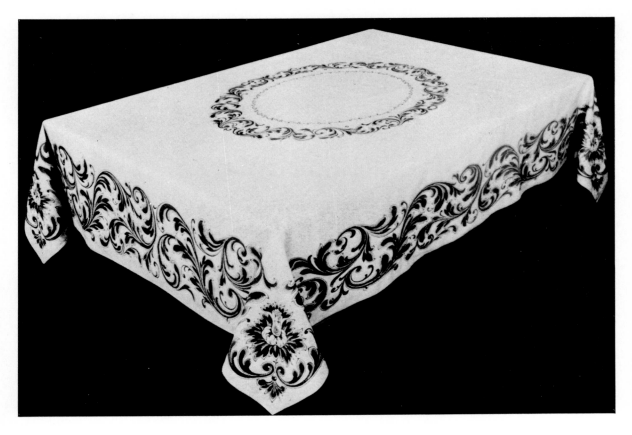

FIGURE 58. ETABS. ABBELOOS & FILS DE GAND

FIGURE 59. ETABS. SOLINTEXT, COURTRAI

FIGURE 60. TISSAGE LA FLANDRE

FIGURE 61. TEXTILES DE WITTE-LIETAER, LAUWE-BIJ-KORTRIJK

FIGURE 62. TEXTILES DE WITTE-LIETAER, LAUWE-BIJ-KORTRIJK

FIGURE 63. S. DOCQUIER, BRUSSELS

FIGURE 64. MANTA S.A., WAASMUNSTER

FIGURE 65. MANTA S.A., WAASMUNSTER

FIGURE 66. S.A. DE WAERSCHOOT, WAERSCHOOT

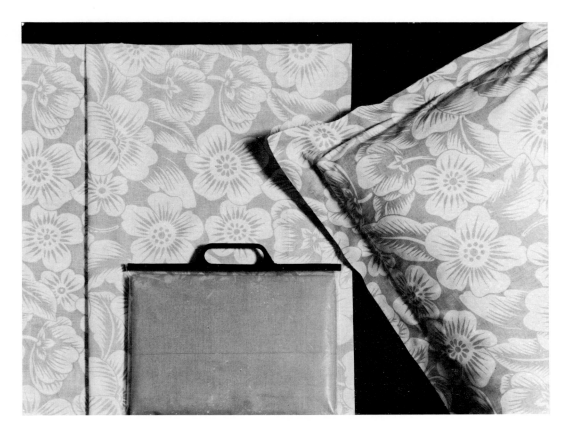

FIGURE 67. U.C.O., LEDEBERG, GHENT

FIGURE 68. S.A. MANTA, WAASMUNSTER

FIGURE 69. S.A. MANTA, WAASMUNSTER

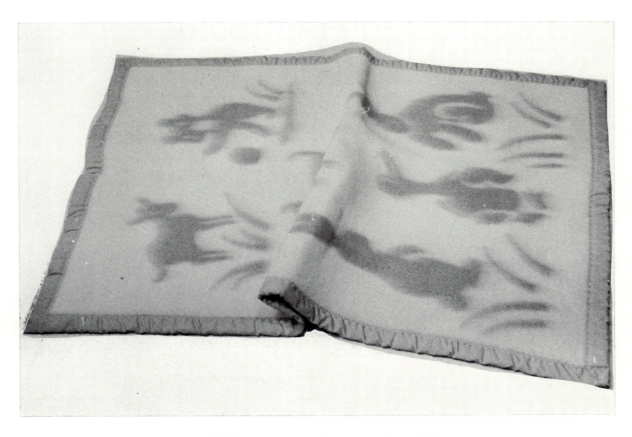

FIGURE 70. S.A. MANTA, WAASMUNSTER

FIGURE 71. ETABS. A. VAN DAMME S.A., EEKLO

FIGURE 72. ETABS. A. VAN DAMME S.A., EEKLO

FIGURE 73. COMBELI, BRUSSELS

FIGURE 74. TISSAGES HOLVOET-VAN OUTRYVE ET LAGAE & FILS

FIGURE 75. TEXIS, BRUSSELS

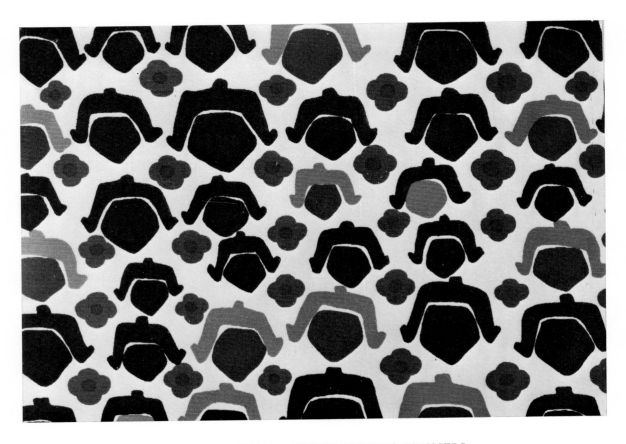

FIGURE 76. ETABS. ATTOUT-SOENENS, BRUSSELS

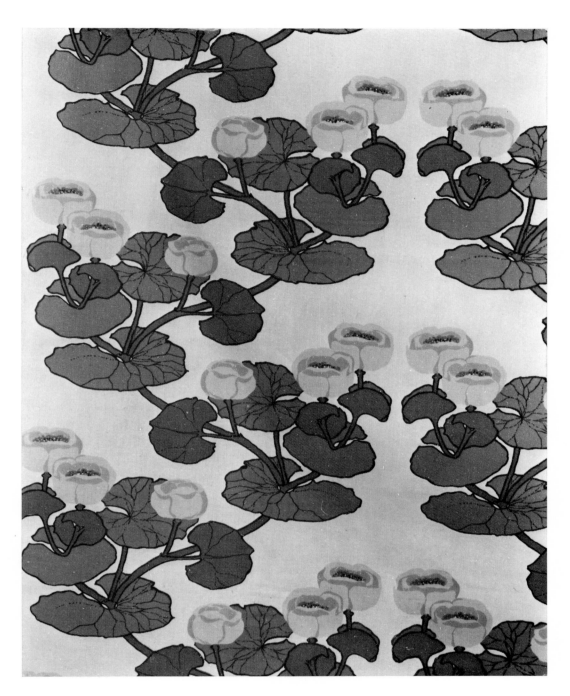

FIGURE 77. ETABS. ATTOUT-SOENENS, BRUSSELS

FIGURE 78. INDIENNERIES BELGES, GHENT

FIGURE 79. INDIENNERIES BELGES, GHENT

FIGURE 80. S.A. LOUTERS, GHENT

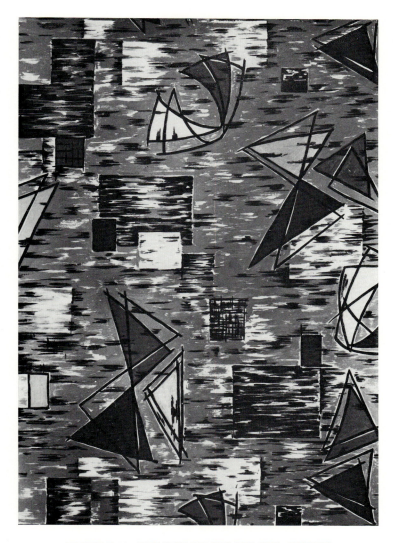

FIGURE 81. INDIENNERIES BELGES, GHENT

FIGURE 82. INDIENNERIES BELGES, GHENT